place photo here

These quotes belong to:

MY Quotable Kid

A Parents' Journal of Unforgettable Quotes

CHRONICLE BOOKS
SAN FRANCISCO

ISBN 978-0-8118-6884-6

Design by Grace Partridge
Typeset in Neutra
Manufactured in China
Chronicle Books endeavors to use environmentally
responsible paper in its gift and stationery products.

10 9

Chronicle Books LLC
680 Second Street
San Francisco, CA 94107
www.chroniclebooks.com

Who:

When:

Age:

Where:

Quote:

Who:

When:

Age:

Where:

Quote:

Quote:

_____

_____

_____

_____

_____

_____

_____

_____

_____

_____

_____

_____

_____

Who: _____

When: _____ Age: _____

Where: _____

_____

Who:

When:

Age:

Where:

Quote:

Quote:

Who:

When:

Age:

Where:

Quote:

Who: ---

When: --

Age: ---

Where: ---

Quote:

Who:

When:

Age:

Where:

Quote:

_____

_____

_____

_____

_____

_____

_____

_____

_____

_____

_____

_____

Who:

When: Age:

Where:

Who:
When:
Age:
Where:

Quote:

Who:

When:

Age:

Where:

Quote:

Quote:

_____

_____

_____

_____

_____

_____

_____

_____

_____

_____

_____

_____

Who: _____

When: _____ Age: _____

Where: _____

_____

Who:

When:

Age:

Where:

Quote:

Quote:

Who:

When:

Age:

Where:

Quote:

_____

_____

_____

_____

_____

_____

_____

_____

_____

_____

_____

Who: _____

When: _____

Age: _____

Where: _____

_____

_____

_____

_____

Quote: _____

_____

_____

_____

_____

_____

_____

_____

_____

_____

_____

_____

_____

_____

_____

_____

_____

_____

Who: _____

When: _____

Age: _____

Where: _____

_____

Quote:

_____
_____
_____
_____
_____
_____
_____
_____
_____
_____
_____
_____
_____

Who: _____

When: _____ Age: _____

Where: _____

_____

Who: _____

When: _____

Age: _____

Where: _____

_____

Quote: _____

_____

_____

_____

_____

_____

_____

_____

_____

_____

_____

_____

_____

_____

Who:

When:

Age:

Where:

Quote:

Quote:

_____

_____

_____

_____

_____

_____

_____

_____

_____

_____

_____

_____

Who:

_____

When: _____ Age: _____

Where:

_____

Who:

When:

Age:

Where:

Quote:

Quote:

Who:

When:

Age:

Where:

Quote:

_____

_____

_____

_____

_____

_____

_____

_____

_____

_____

_____

_____

Who: _____

When: _____

Age: _____

Where: _____

_____

_____

_____

_____

_____

_____

Quote:

_____
_____
_____
_____
_____
_____
_____
_____
_____
_____
_____

Who: _____

When: _____

Age: _____

Where: _____

_____

_____
_____
_____
_____
_____
_____
_____
_____
_____
_____
_____

Quote:

_____

_____

_____

_____

_____

_____

_____

_____

_____

_____

_____

_____

Who:

When: Age:

Where:

Who:
When:
Age:
Where:

Quote:

Who:

When:

Age:

Where:

Quote:

Quote:

_____

_____

_____

_____

_____

_____

_____

_____

_____

_____

_____

_____

Who:
_____

When: _____ Age: _____

Where:
_____

_____

Who:

When:

Age:

Where:

Quote:

Quote:

Who:

When:

Age:

Where:

Quote:

Who:

When:

Age:

Where:

Quote:

_____

_____

_____

_____

_____

_____

_____

_____

_____

_____

_____

_____

_____

_____

_____

_____

_____

_____

Who:

When:

Age:

Where:

_____

Quote:
_____

_____

_____

_____

_____

_____

_____

_____

_____

_____

_____

_____

_____

Who:
_____
When: Age:
_____
Where:
_____
_____

Who:

When:

Age:

Where:

Quote:

Who: ....

When: ....

Age: ....

Where: ....

....

....

Quote: ....

....

....

....

....

....

....

....

Quote:

Who:

When: Age:

Where:

Who:

When:

Age:

Where:

Quote:

Quote:

Who:

When:

Age:

Where:

Quote:

_____

_____

_____

_____

_____

_____

_____

_____

_____

_____

_____

_____

Who: _____

When: _____

Age: _____

Where: _____

_____

_____

_____

_____

_____

Quote:

_____
_____
_____
_____
_____
_____
_____
_____
_____
_____
_____
_____
_____
_____
_____
_____
_____
_____
_____
_____
_____

Who:
_____
When:
_____
Age:
_____
Where:
_____
_____

Quote:

_____

_____

_____

_____

_____

_____

_____

_____

_____

_____

_____

_____

Who:
_____

When: _____ Age: _____

Where:
_____

_____

Who:

When:

Age:

Where:

Quote:

Who:

When:

Age:

Where:

Quote:

Quote: _____
_____
_____
_____
_____
_____
_____
_____
_____
_____
_____
_____
_____
_____

Who: _____
When: _____ Age: _____
Where: _____
_____

Who:

When:

Age:

Where:

Quote:

Quote:

Who:
When:
Age:
Where:

Quote:

_____

_____

_____

_____

_____

_____

_____

_____

_____

_____

_____

_____

_____

Who: _____

When: _____

Age: _____

Where: _____

_____

_____

_____

_____

_____

_____

Quote:

Who:

When:

Age:

Where:

Quote:

_____

_____

_____

_____

_____

_____

_____

_____

_____

_____

_____

_____

_____

Who: _____

When: _____ Age: _____

Where: _____

_____

Who:

When:

Age:

Where:

Quote:

Who:

When:

Age:

Where:

Quote:

Quote:

Who:

When: Age:

Where:

Who:

When:

Age:

Where:

Quote:

Quote:

Who:

When:

Age:

Where:

Quote:

Who:

When:

Age:

Where:

Quote:

Who:

When:

Age:

Where:

Quote:

_____

_____

_____

_____

_____

_____

_____

_____

_____

_____

_____

_____

Who:
_____
When: _____ Age: _____
_____
Where:
_____
_____

Who:

When:

Age:

Where:

Quote:

Who:

When:

Age:

Where:

Quote:

Quote:

_____

_____

_____

_____

_____

_____

_____

_____

_____

_____

_____

Who: _____

When: _____ Age: _____

Where: _____

_____

Who:

When:

Age:

Where:

Quote:

Quote:

Who:

When:

Age:

Where:

Quote:

Who:

When:

Age:

Where:

Quote:

Who:

When:

Age:

Where:

Quote:

_____

_____

_____

_____

_____

_____

_____

_____

_____

_____

_____

_____

Who:
_____
When: Age:
_____
Where:
_____

_____

Who:

When:

Age:

Where:

Quote:

Who:

When:

Age:

Where:

Quote:

Quote:
_____
_____
_____
_____
_____
_____
_____
_____
_____
_____
_____
_____
_____

Who:
_____
When: _____ Age: _____
Where:
_____
_____

Who:

When:

Age:

Where:

Quote:

Quote:

Who:

When:

Age:

Where:

Quote:

_____

_____

_____

_____

_____

_____

_____

_____

_____

_____

_____

_____

_____

Who: _____

When: _____

Age: _____

Where: _____

_____

Quote:

_____

_____

_____

_____

_____

_____

_____

_____

_____

_____

_____

_____

_____

_____

_____

_____

_____

_____

_____

_____

_____

Who: _____

When: _____

Age: _____

Where: _____

_____

Quote:

_____
_____
_____
_____
_____
_____
_____
_____
_____
_____
_____
_____
_____

Who:
_____
When: Age:
_____
Where:
_____
_____

Who:

When:

Age:

Where:

Quote:

Who:

When:

Age:

Where:

Quote:

Quote:
_____
_____
_____
_____
_____
_____
_____
_____
_____
_____
_____
_____
_____

Who:
_____
When: _____ Age: _____
Where:
_____

Who:

When:

Age:

Where:

Quote:

Quote:

_____

_____

_____

_____

_____

_____

_____

_____

_____

_____

_____

_____

_____

Who: _____

When: _____

Age: _____

Where: _____

_____

_____

Quote:

_____

_____

_____

_____

_____

_____

_____

_____

_____

_____

_____

Who: _____

When: _____

Age: _____

Where: _____

_____

_____

_____

_____

_____

Quote: _____

_____

_____

_____

_____

_____

_____

_____

_____

_____

_____

_____

_____

_____

_____

_____

_____

_____

_____

_____

Who: _____

When: _____

Age: _____

Where: _____

_____

Quote:

_____

_____

_____

_____

_____

_____

_____

_____

_____

_____

_____

_____

Who:

When: Age:

Where:

Who:

When:

Age:

Where:

Quote:

Who: ....

When: ....

Age: ....

Where: ....

....

....

Quote: ....

....

....

....

....

....

....

....

Quote:

Who:

When: Age:

Where:

Who:

When:

Age:

Where:

Quote:

Quote:

Who:
When:
Age:
Where:

Quote:

_____

_____

_____

_____

_____

_____

_____

_____

_____

_____

_____

_____

Who: _____

When: _____

Age: _____

Where: _____

_____

_____

_____

_____

_____

_____

Quote:

_____

_____

_____

_____

_____

_____

_____

_____

_____

_____

_____

_____

_____

_____

_____

_____

_____

_____

_____

_____

_____

Who:

_____

When:

_____

Age:

_____

Where:

_____

_____

Quote:

_____
_____
_____
_____
_____
_____
_____
_____
_____
_____
_____
_____
_____

Who: _____

When: _____ Age: _____

Where: _____

_____

Who:
....

When:
....

Age:
....

Where:
....

....

Quote:
....

....

....

....

....

....

....

....

....

....

....

....

....

....

Who:

When:

Age:

Where:

Quote:

Quote:
_____
_____
_____
_____
_____
_____
_____
_____
_____
_____
_____
_____

Who: _____

When: _____ Age: _____

Where: _____
_____

Who:

When:

Age:

Where:

Quote:

Quote:

Who:

When:

Age:

Where:

Quote:

_____

_____

_____

_____

_____

_____

_____

_____

_____

_____

_____

Who: _____

When: _____

Age: _____

Where: _____

_____

_____

_____

_____

Quote:

Who:

When:

Age:

Where:

Quote:

_____
_____
_____
_____
_____
_____
_____
_____
_____
_____
_____
_____
_____

Who:
When: Age:
Where:

Who:

When:

Age:

Where:

Quote:

Who:

When:

Age:

Where:

Quote:

Quote:
_____
_____
_____
_____
_____
_____
_____
_____
_____
_____
_____
_____
_____

Who: _____

When: _____ Age: _____

Where: _____

_____

Who:

When:

Age:

Where:

Quote:

Quote:

Who:

When:

Age:

Where:

Quote:

_____

_____

_____

_____

_____

_____

_____

_____

_____

_____

_____

_____

Who: _____

When: _____

Age: _____

Where: _____

_____

_____

_____

_____

_____

Quote:
....

....

....

....

....

....

....

....

....

....

....

....

....

....

....

....

....

....

....

....

Who: ....

When: ....

Age: ....

Where: ....

....

Quote:

_____

_____

_____

_____

_____

_____

_____

_____

_____

_____

_____

_____

Who:
_____
When: Age:
_____
Where:
_____

_____

Who:

When:

Age:

Where:

Quote:

Who: _____

When: _____

Age: _____

Where: _____

_____

_____

Quote: _____

_____

_____

_____

_____

_____

_____

_____

Quote:
_____
_____
_____
_____
_____
_____
_____
_____
_____
_____
_____
_____
_____

Who: _____

When: _____ Age: _____

Where: _____

_____

Who:

When:

Age:

Where:

Quote:

Quote:

Who:

When:

Age:

Where:

Quote:

_____

_____

_____

_____

_____

_____

_____

_____

_____

_____

Who: _____

When: _____

Age: _____

Where: _____

_____

_____

_____

_____

_____

Quote: _____
_____
_____
_____
_____
_____
_____
_____
_____
_____

Who: _____
When: _____
Age: _____
Where: _____
_____

_____
_____
_____
_____
_____
_____
_____
_____
_____
_____
_____
_____
_____
_____
_____

Quote:
_____
_____
_____
_____
_____
_____
_____
_____
_____
_____
_____
_____
_____

Who: _____
When: _____ Age: _____
Where: _____
_____

Who:

When:

Age:

Where:

Quote:

Quote:

Who:

When: Age:

Where:

Who:

When:

Age:

Where:

Quote:

Quote:

Who:

When:

Age:

Where:

Quote:

Who:

When:

Age:

Where:

Quote:

Who:

When:

Age:

Where:

Quote:

_____

_____

_____

_____

_____

_____

_____

_____

_____

_____

_____

_____

Who:
_____

When: Age:
_____

Where:
_____

Who:

When:

Age:

Where:

Quote:

Who: ----------------------------------

When: ---------------------------------

Age: ----------------------------------

Where: --------------------------------

Quote: --------------------------------

Quote:

_____

_____

_____

_____

_____

_____

_____

_____

_____

_____

_____

_____

Who: _____

When: _____ Age: _____

Where: _____

_____

Who:

When:

Age:

Where:

Quote:

Quote:

Who:

When:

Age:

Where:

Quote:

_____

_____

_____

_____

_____

_____

_____

_____

_____

_____

_____

Who:

When:

Age:

Where:

_____

_____

_____

_____

Quote: ....

....

....

....

....

....

....

....

....

....

....

....

....

....

....

....

....

....

....

....

....

....

....

Who: ....

When: ....

Age: ....

Where: ....

....

Quote: _____
_____
_____
_____
_____
_____
_____
_____
_____
_____
_____
_____
_____
_____

Who: _____
When: _____ Age: _____
Where: _____
_____

Who:

When:

Age:

Where:

Quote:

Who:

When:

Age:

Where:

Quote:

Quote:
_____
_____
_____
_____
_____
_____
_____
_____
_____
_____
_____
_____

Who:
_____
When: _____ Age: _____
Where:
_____

Who:

When:

Age:

Where:

Quote:

Quote:

Who:

When:

Age:

Where:

Quote:

Who:

When:

Age:

Where:

Quote:

Who:

When:

Age:

Where:

Quote:

Who:

When: Age:

Where:

Who: _____

When: _____

Age: _____

Where: _____

_____

Quote: _____

_____

_____

_____

_____

_____

_____

_____

_____

_____

_____

_____

_____

_____

Who:
When:
Age:

Where:

Quote:

Quote:

_____

_____

_____

_____

_____

_____

_____

_____

_____

_____

_____

_____

Who:
_____

When: _____ Age: _____

Where:
_____

_____

Who:

When:

Age:

Where:

Quote: